Corrupted Coloring Book

(Not for Kids, Only for Adults)

Dark sense of humor that adults can easily appreciate

Vol. 1

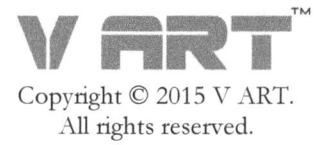

HOW TO CREATE MORBIDLY FUNNY COLORING BOOKS FOR ADULTS

Coloring books for adults have been a growing trend for a number of years. This trend is so popular to the extent that there are several mobile app with ready-made coloring pages suited to adults. They are a fantastic way to unwind from the tension and adult worries of this world. For those who are in creative fields or those just looking to channel some inspiration, coloring books are a great way to get the juices flowing.

In the same vein of creativity, is corrupting coloring books themed for children and making them suit the more macabre or dark sense of humor that adults can easily appreciate. In as much as it would be a great laugh to color a book that already has a zombie little mermaid, they are not available for purchase.

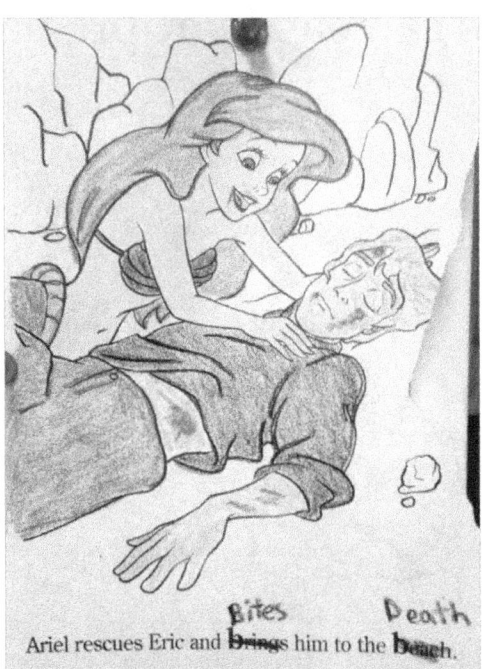

Bites   Death
Ariel rescues Eric and ~~brings~~ him to the ~~beach~~.

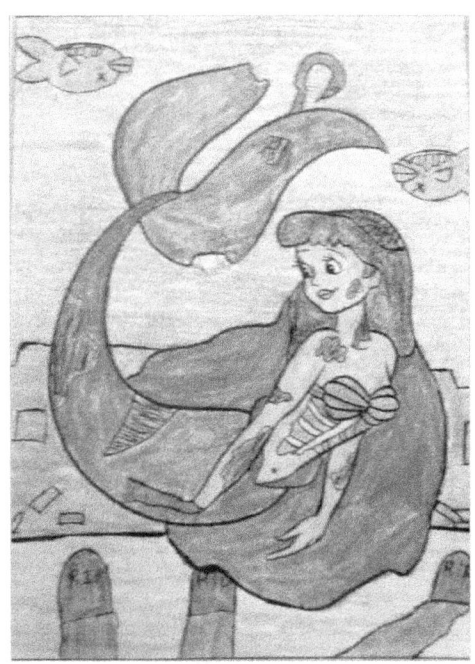

The only way is to create them for yourself.

THE PROCESS

1. **Collect your material**

    Here, your material essentially means the coloring pages. Unless you are a good illustrator who can visualize and draw a child friendly images then corrupt them, you're going to need your scrap book skills. If you have kids, nephews, nieces or children that you babysit then you can borrow a few leafs from their coloring books. Alternatively, you could just go out and buy your own children's coloring book.

2. **Go online**

    If you can't find any interesting images in the coloring books at hand, you can search online. There are plenty of resources online. From free to paid products, you can browse a wide variety of images from full drawings to those that require you to finish the drawing. The finish-the-drawing pages are great because they allow you to create a split personality type of drawing. Once you have selected the pages you want, you can either edit them digitally or print them out and draw on them physically.

3. Spot the Perfect drawing

How do you know whether or not the drawings that you have chosen will make a deliciously funny adult drawing? The key is in the little things. Look at the pose that the character in the story has. Are they bending over someone in a manner that could be murderous? Could that uplifted hand hold a knife ready to stab? Could those eyebrows be curved into an evil facial expression with the stroke of a sharpie? You have to open up your mind and welcome in all those deviant thoughts so that you can see all the incongruous bits in a seemingly innocuous children's drawing.

Take for example this sheriff turned into a failed psychopath:

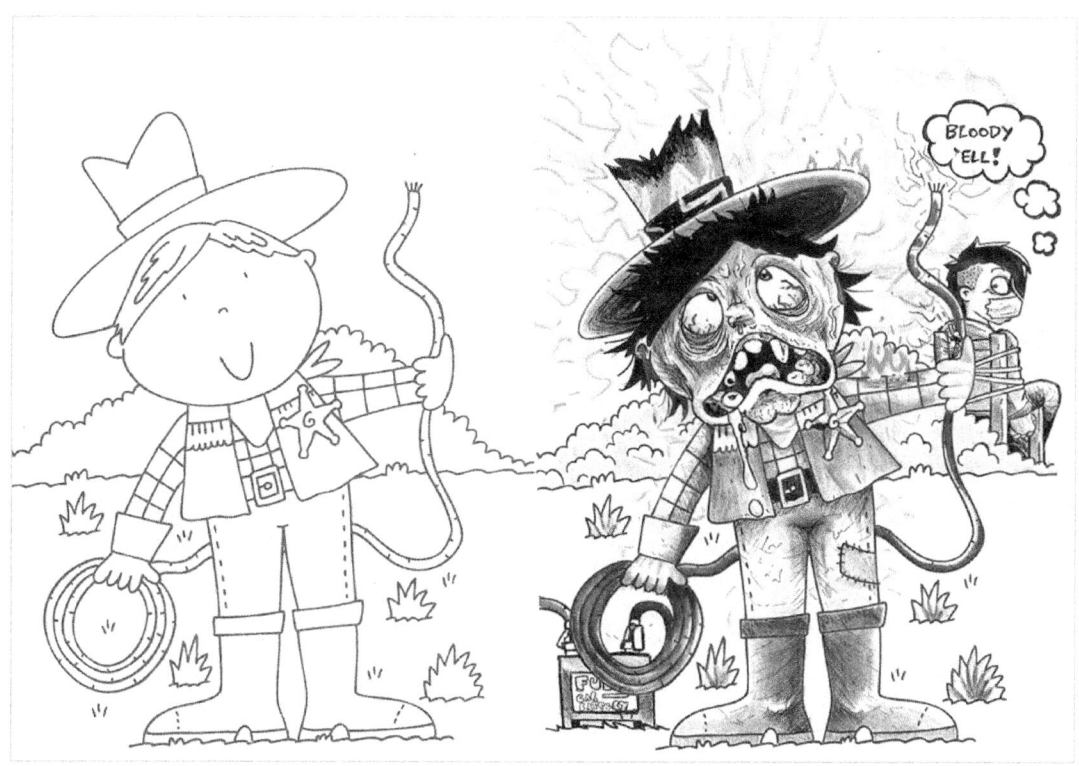

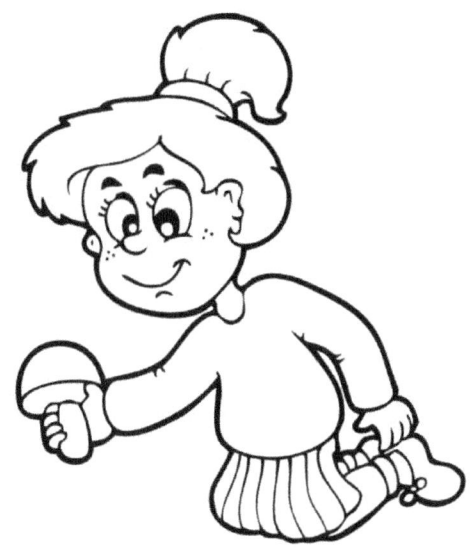
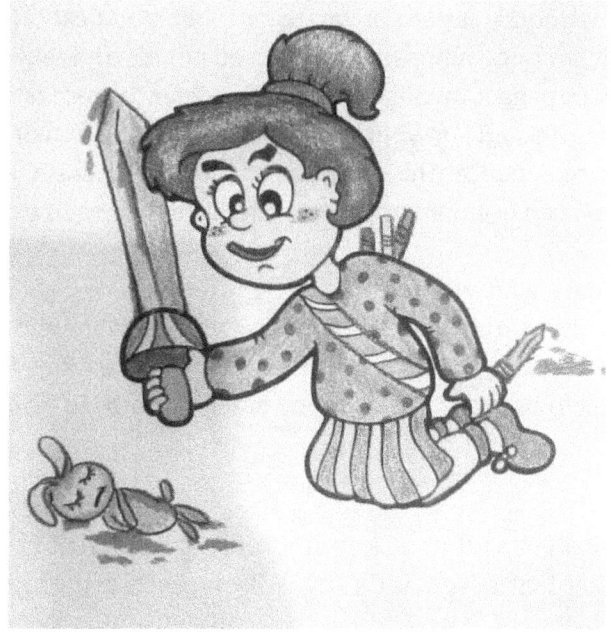

Another example for a little girl.

4. **Tools for drawing**

Once you have your perfect drawing, there are two options on how to edit them. You can either do it digitally or manually. If the page was printed out you can scan it back into your computer to edit digitally. There are a number of programs that you can use to do this. The simplest program is Windows Paint which is in every PC. The best thing about paint is that it is so easy to use you do not need a tutorial. If you want to do a perfect job that you would be proud to show off, you can use more sophisticated programs like Corel Draw, Adobe InDesign and Photoshop. The last tool you can use to draw are online photo and image editing websites that are free to use and offer you a lot of effects to play with. An example is Pic Monkey.

If you wish to illustrate manually, your drawing needs to be bold black and white. You may need to sketch softly with pencil first before going over with a black marker, sharpie or ink pen. Once you're done drawing manually, you need to scan and print out the finished drawing just so that you get a clean, neat page.

5. **Keep it simple**

The key to achieving the perfect morbidly funny coloring book for adults is simplicity. Keep your ideas simple. Most coloring books are appealing due to their simple line drawings and uncluttered compositions. Therefore, whatever ad lib you choose, keep the lines simple and the added illustrations to a minimum. This will ensure that the finished product looks natural. The second benefit of keeping your changes to a minimum is that it will be easier to achieve.

6. **Color the changes**

Sometimes, the composition is so perfect that you don't need to draw on it you can just go in and color in the zombie lesions or whatever other modifications you may have.
Break out your crayons or colored pencils and take your time putting in the needed colors and effects on your page. Crayons will give you bolder colors, faster while colored pencils give a cleaner finish. A clever tip to tidying up your crayon work is to take a ruler, hold it perpendicular to the page and scrape the excess wax of. This gives you an interesting finish. If you want to further highlight and shadow your work you can use marker pens which make the shadows stand out in stark relief.

7. **Share your work**

Being morbidly funny is no fun if you don't share it with other people. There is a site called Coloring Book Corruptions where you can submit your creations for the entertainment of others. Alternatively create a micro blog on Tumblr or any other platform to display your warped creativity.

At the end day what is key in creating an adult coloring book in having fun and channeling you inner naughtiness. That's the only way to see what others don't see and to create a truly funny work of art.

Credit

Images: http://coloringbookcorruptions.com/

Information: http://www.craftsy.com/blog/2015/05/how-to-make-a-coloring-book/

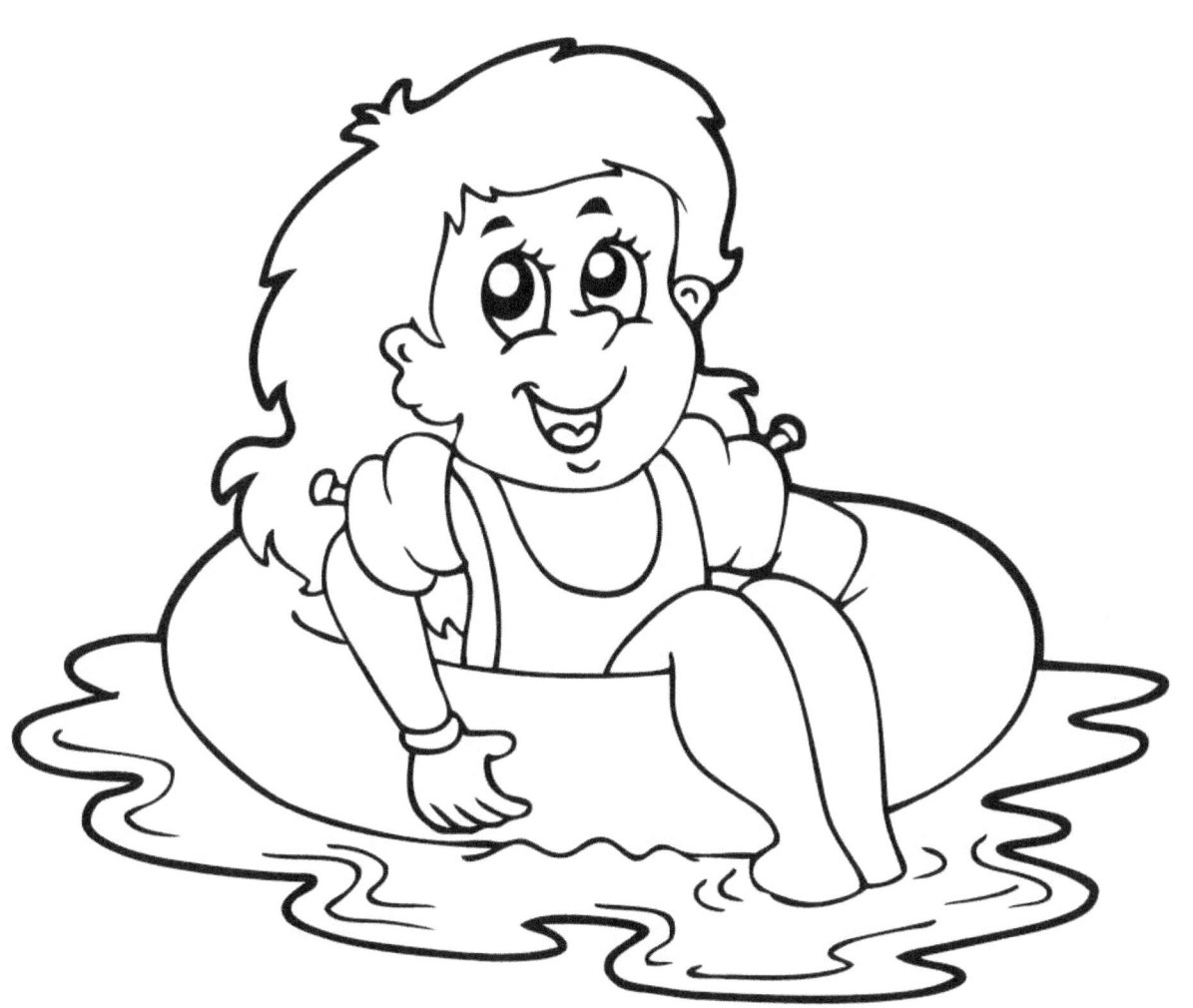

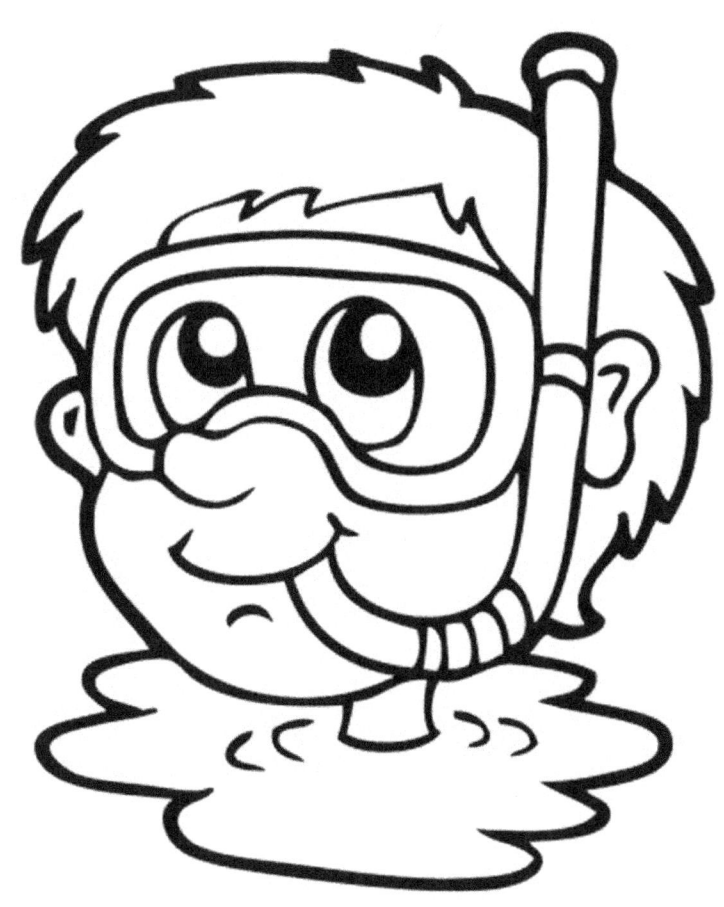

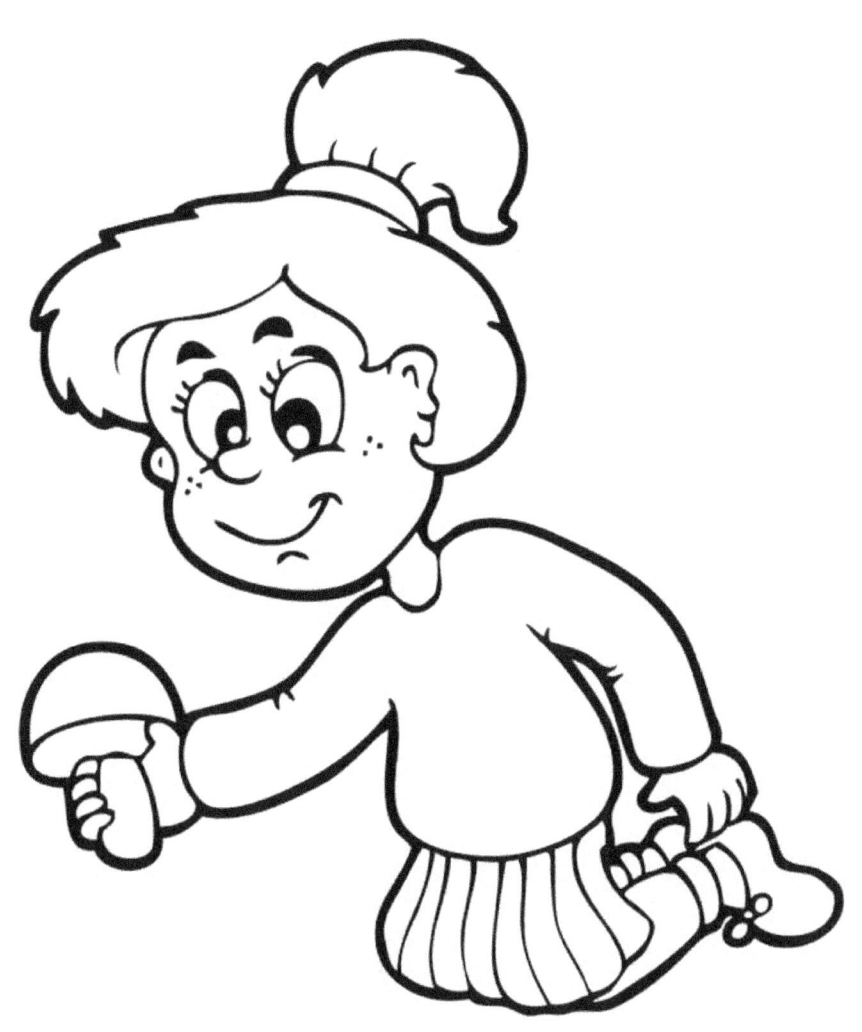

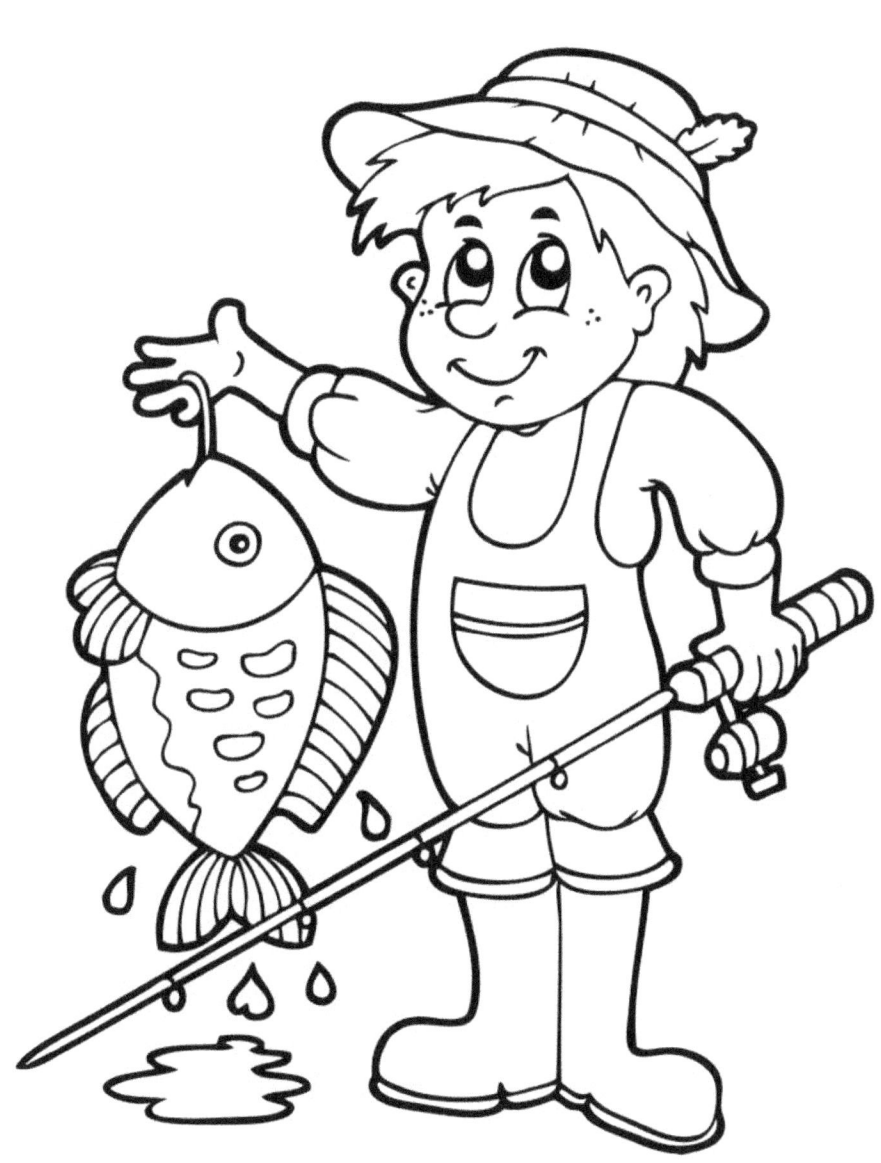

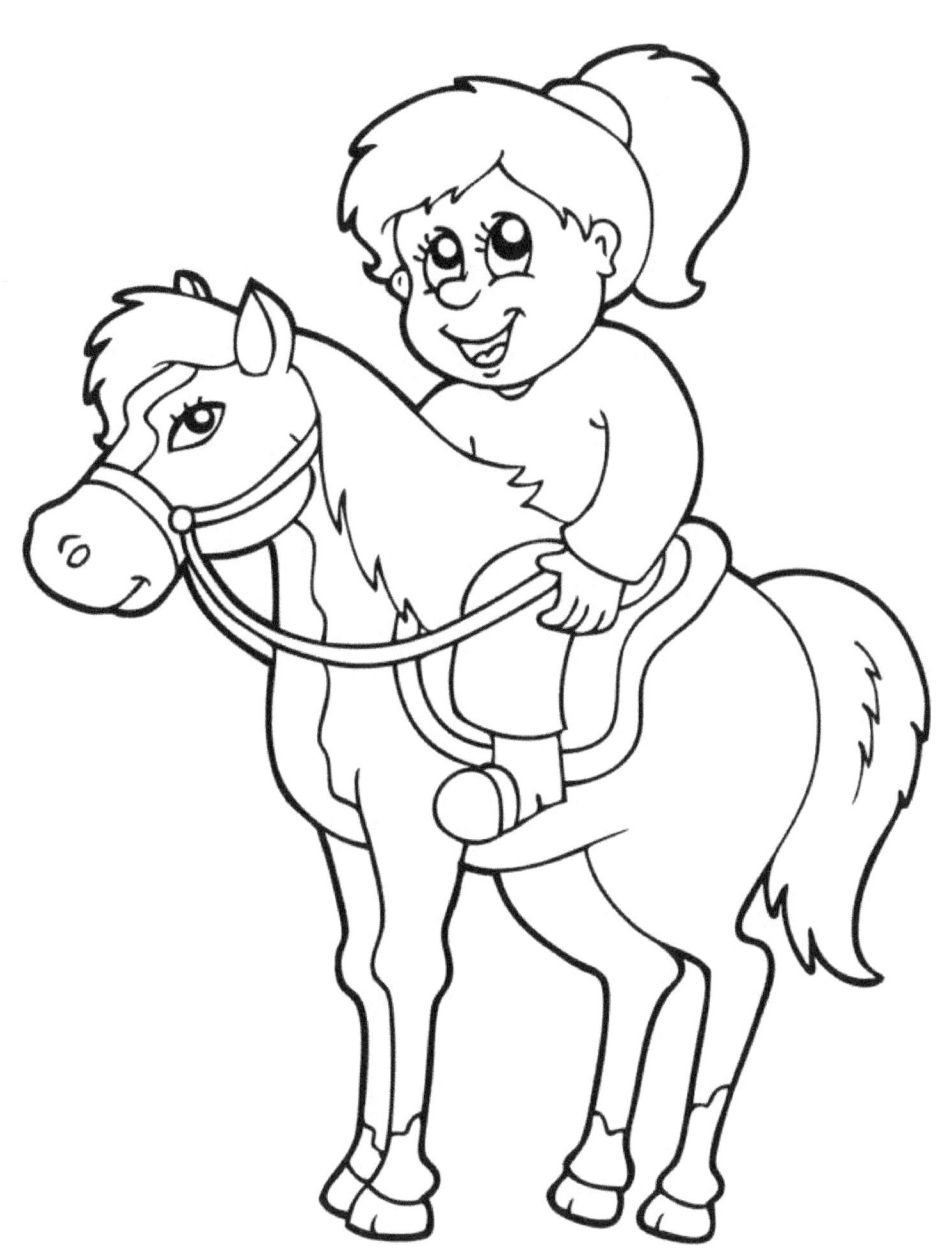

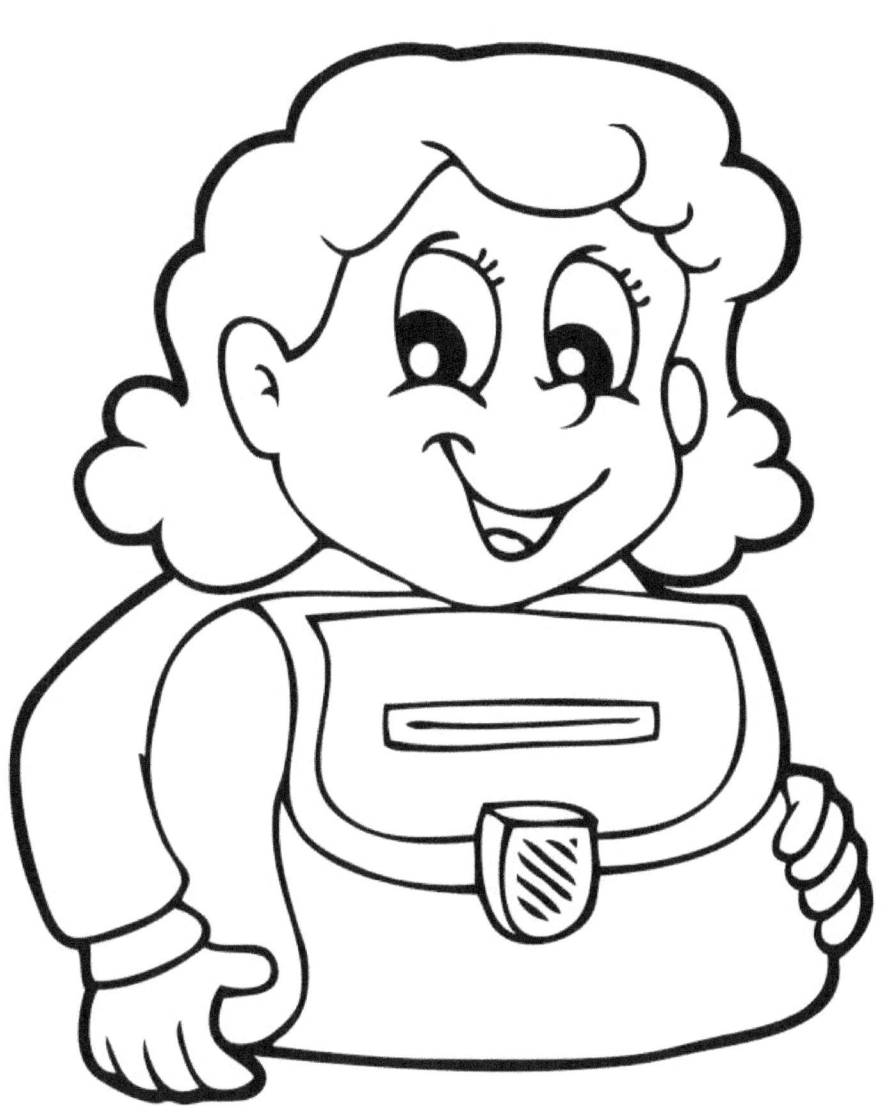

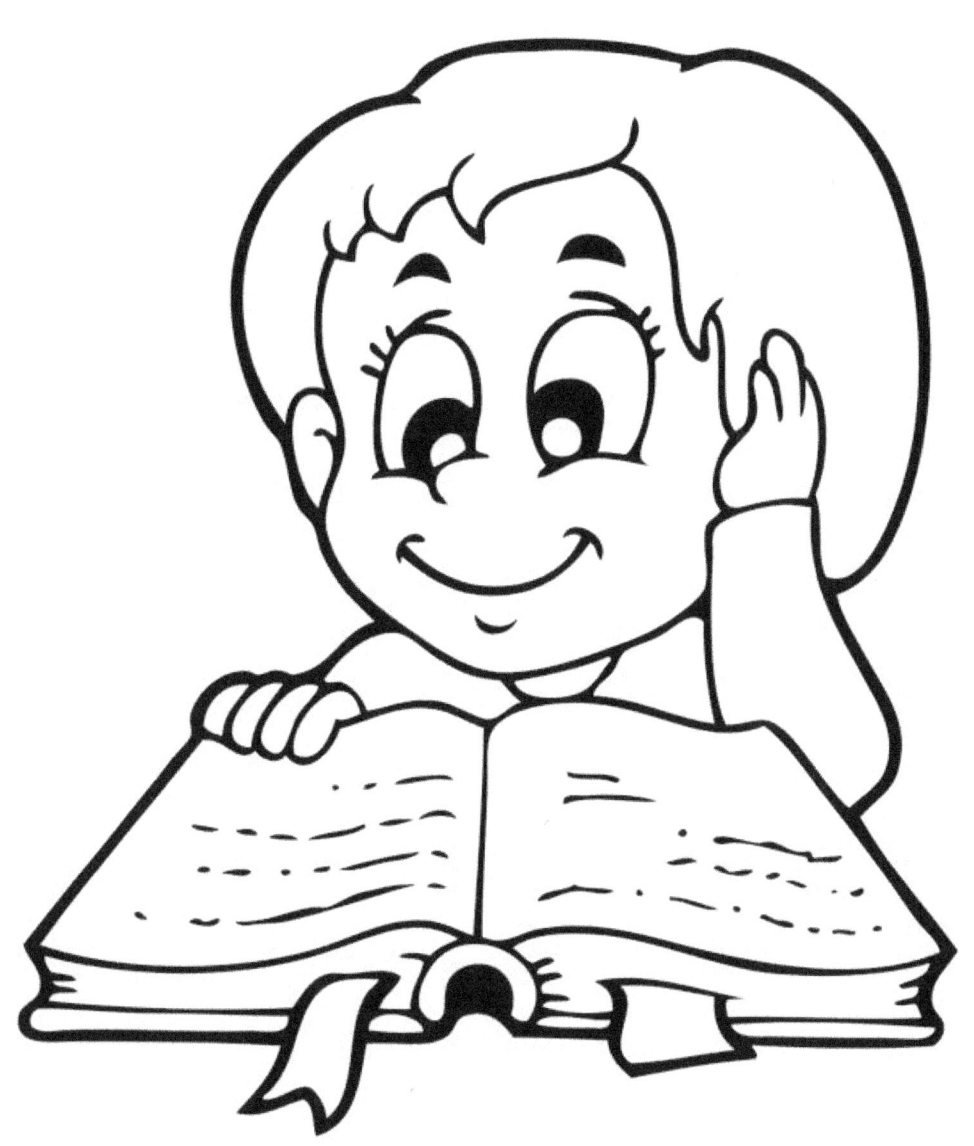

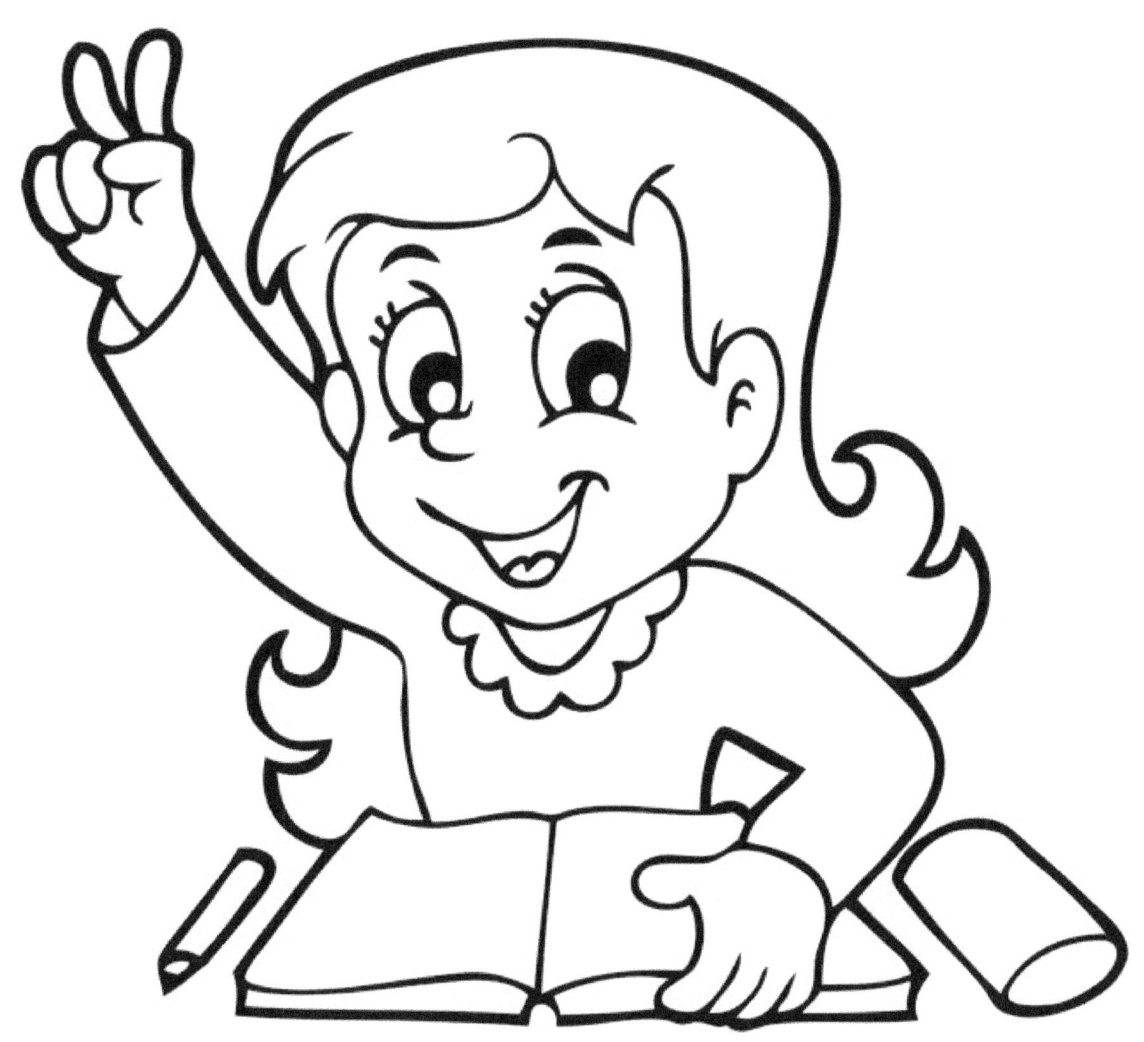

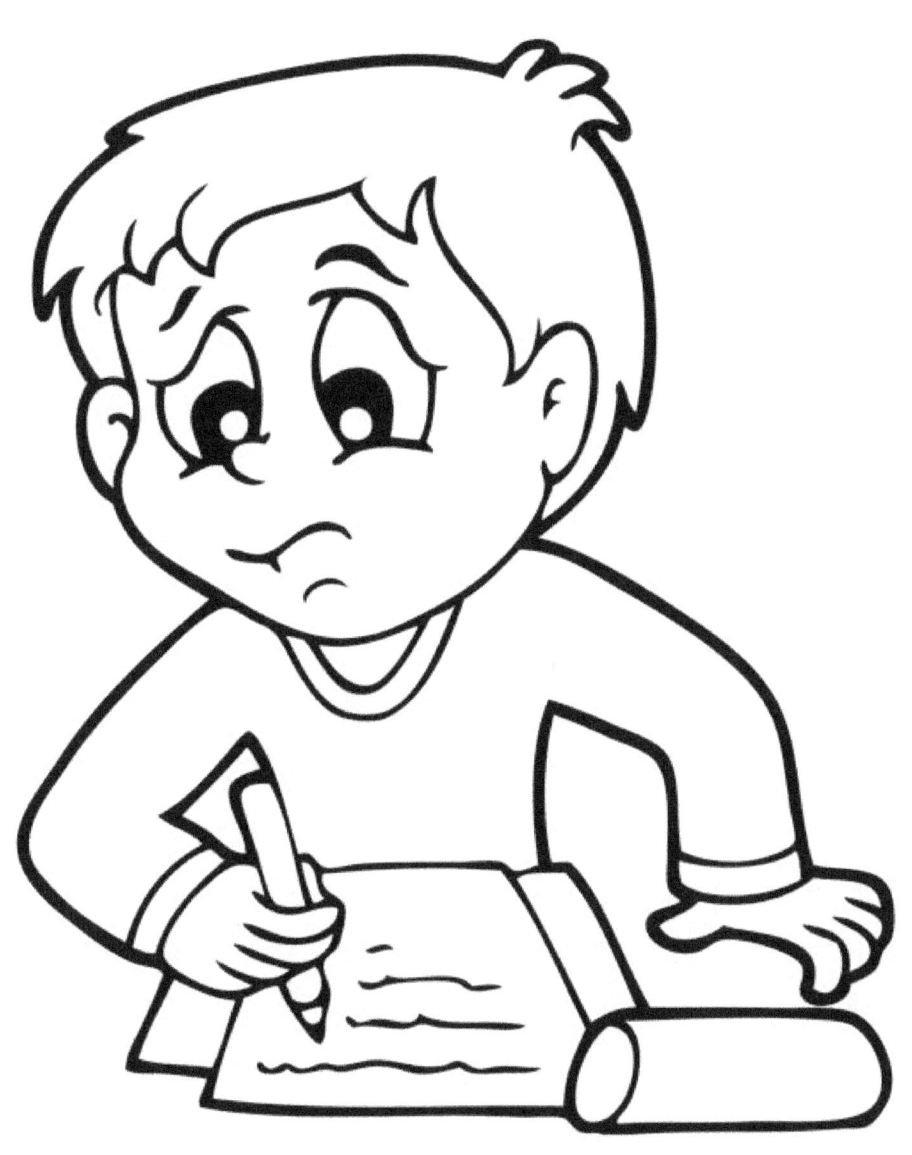

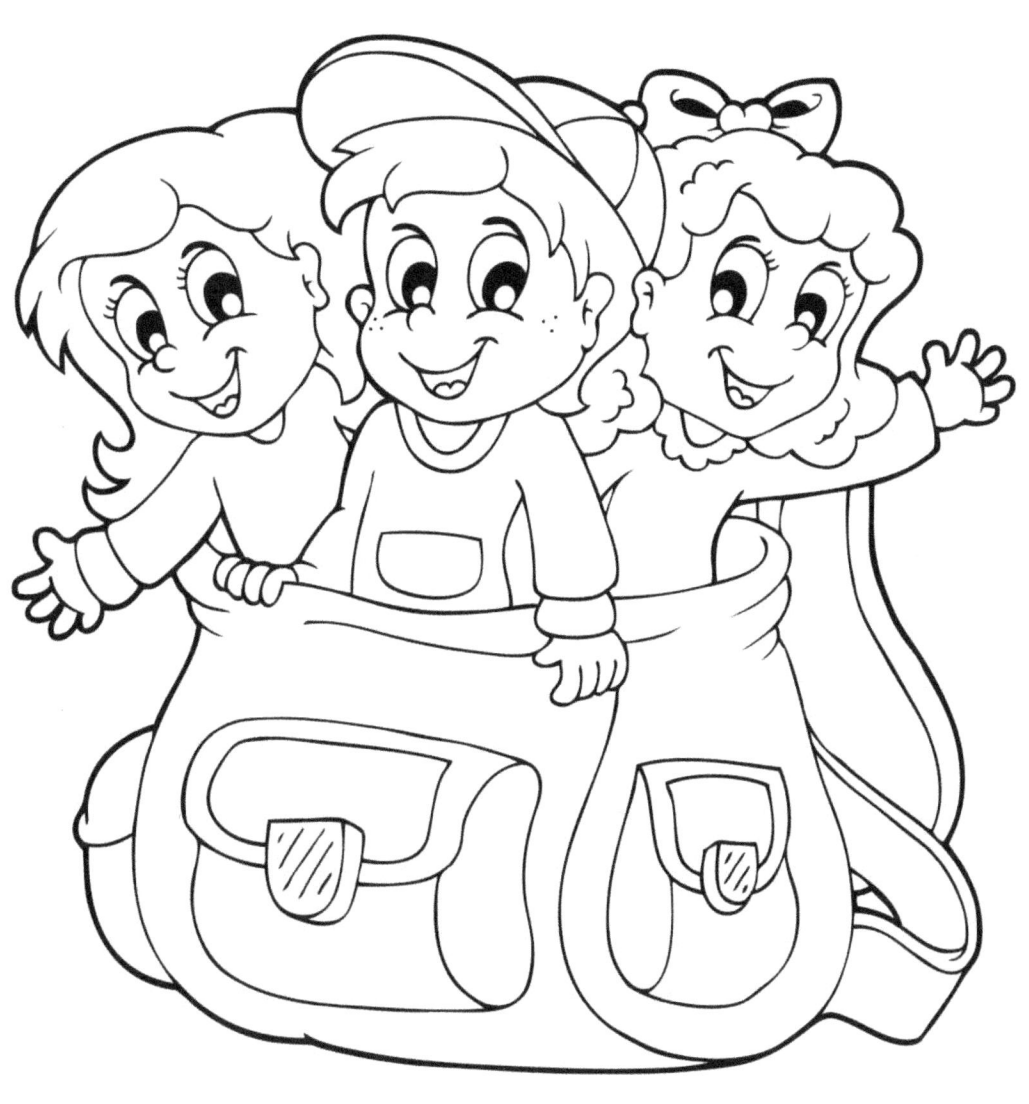

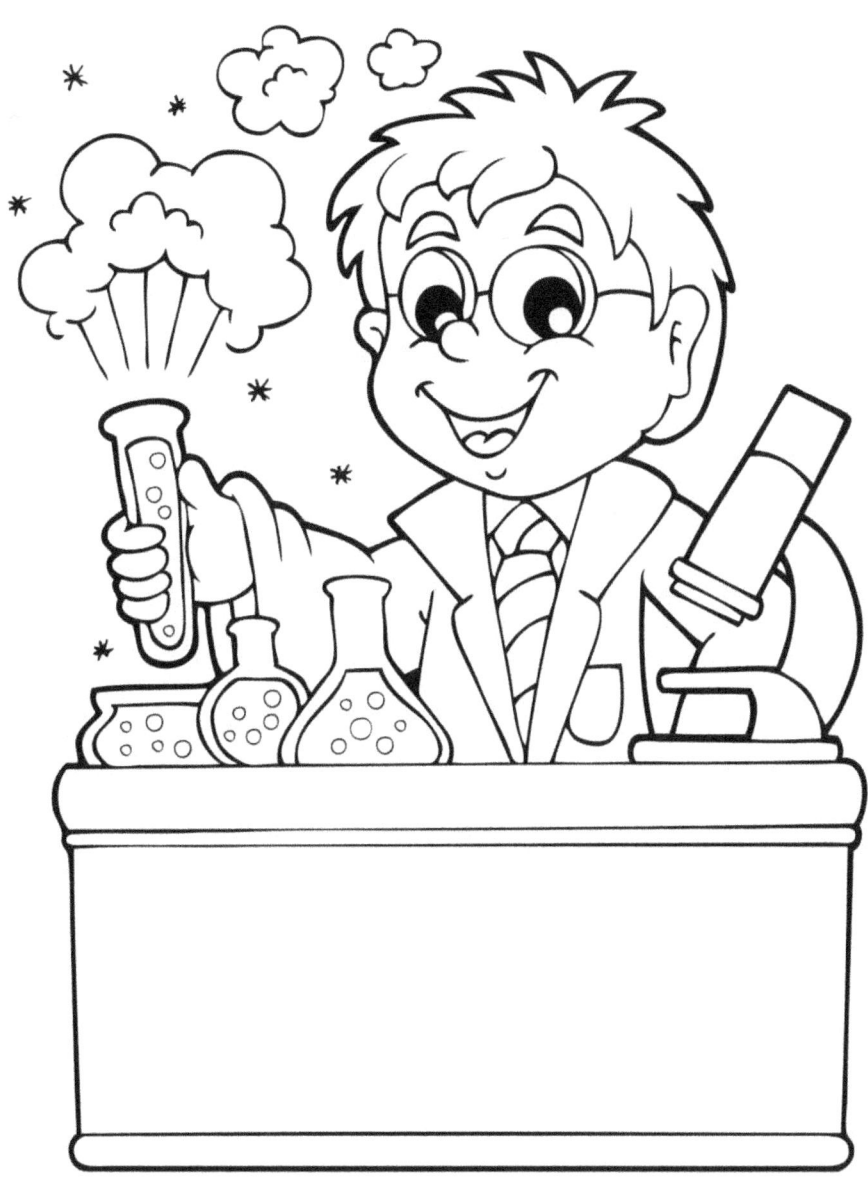

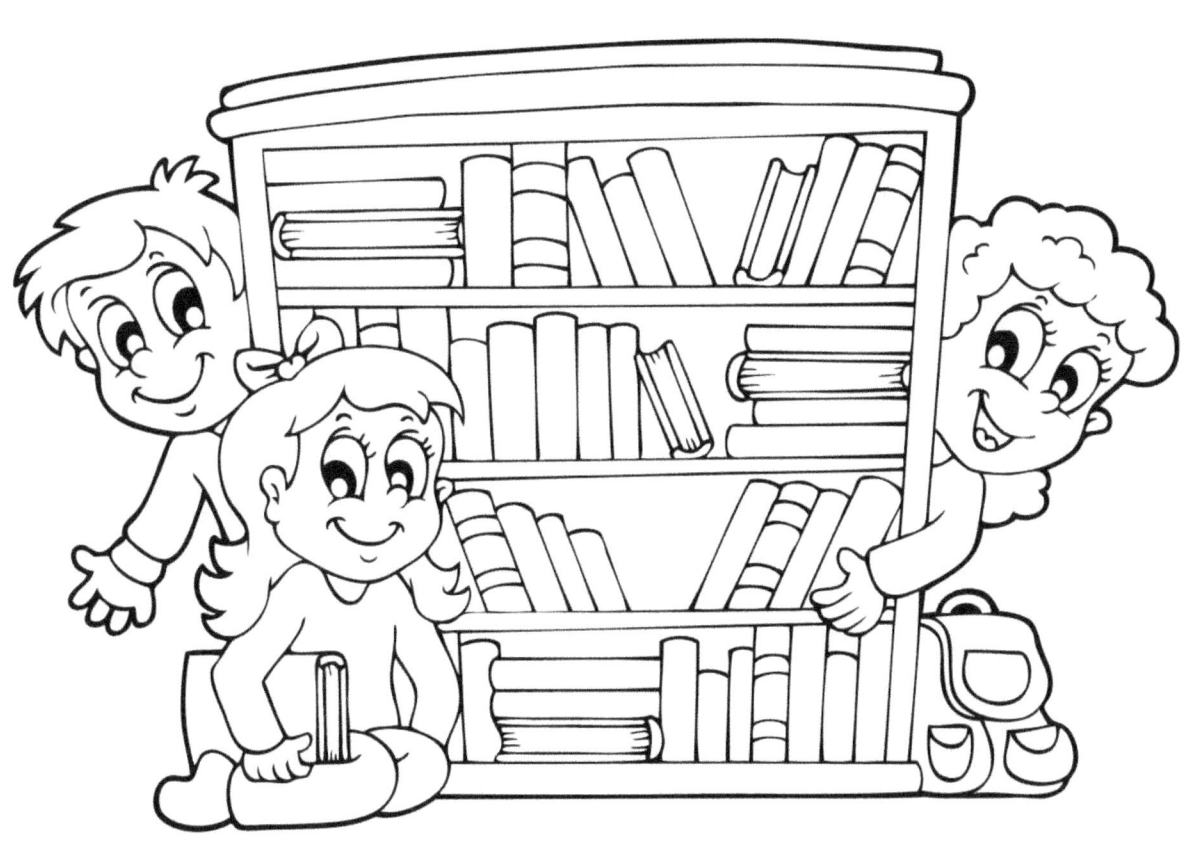

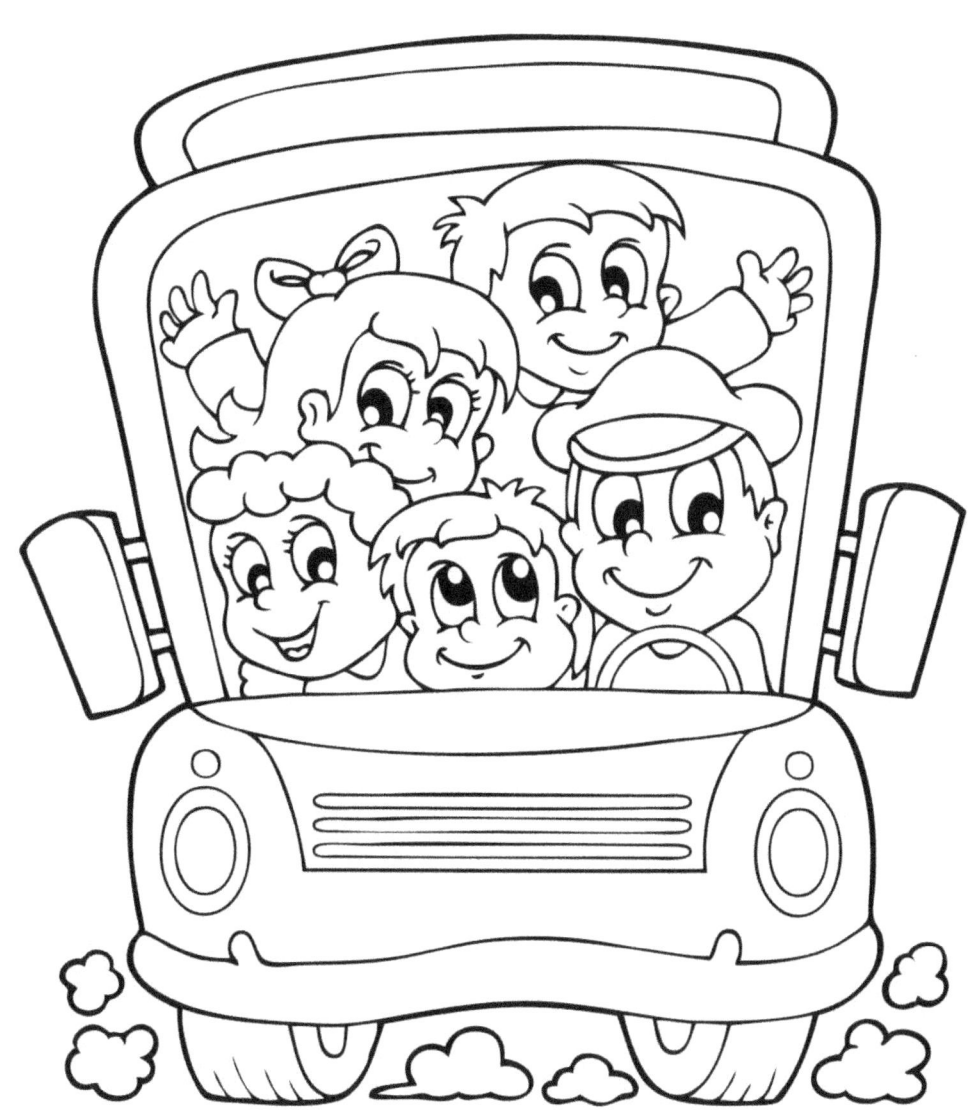

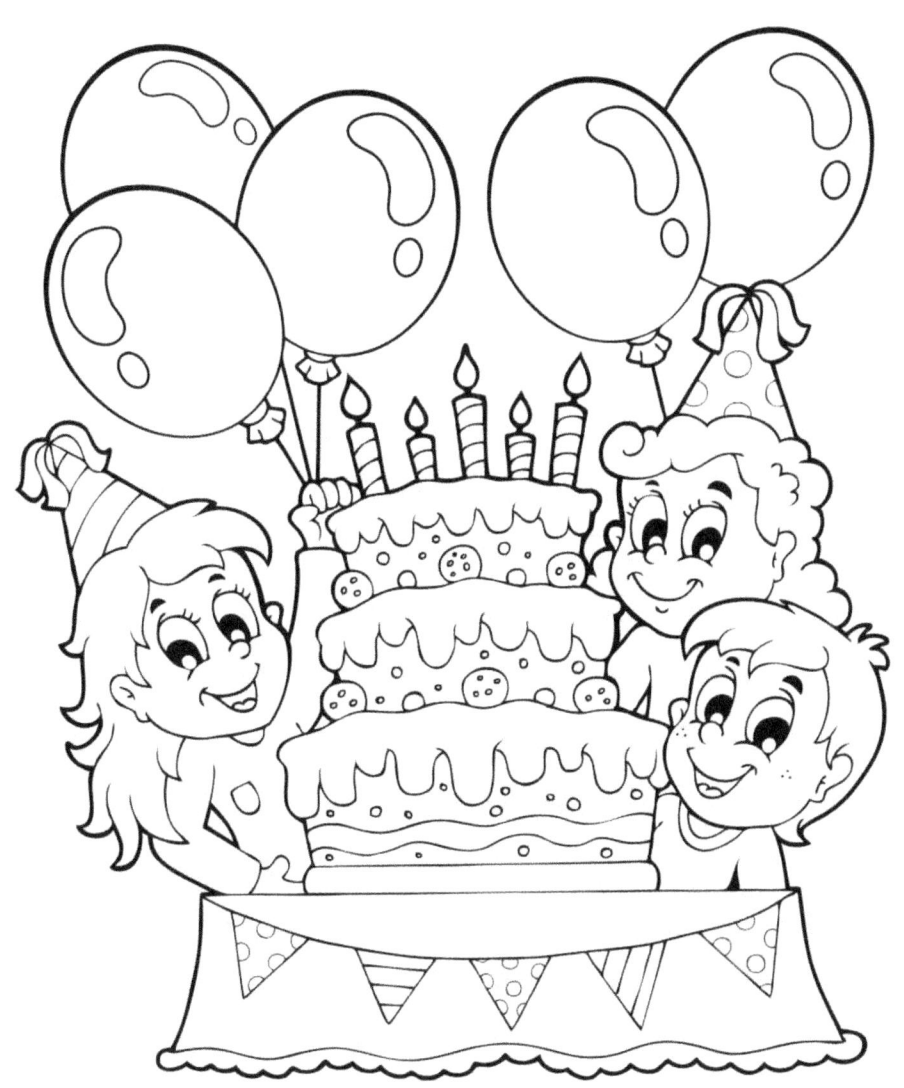

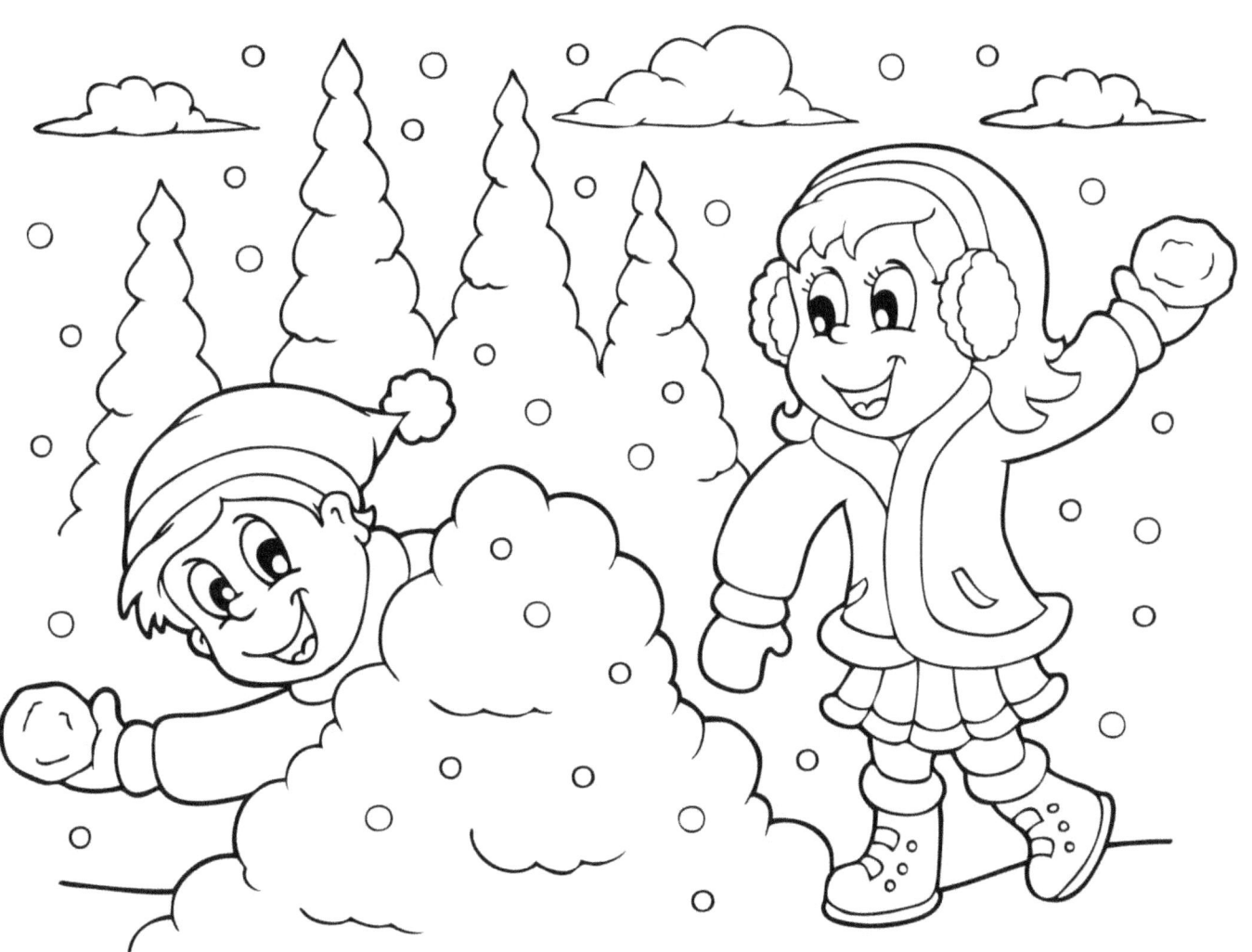

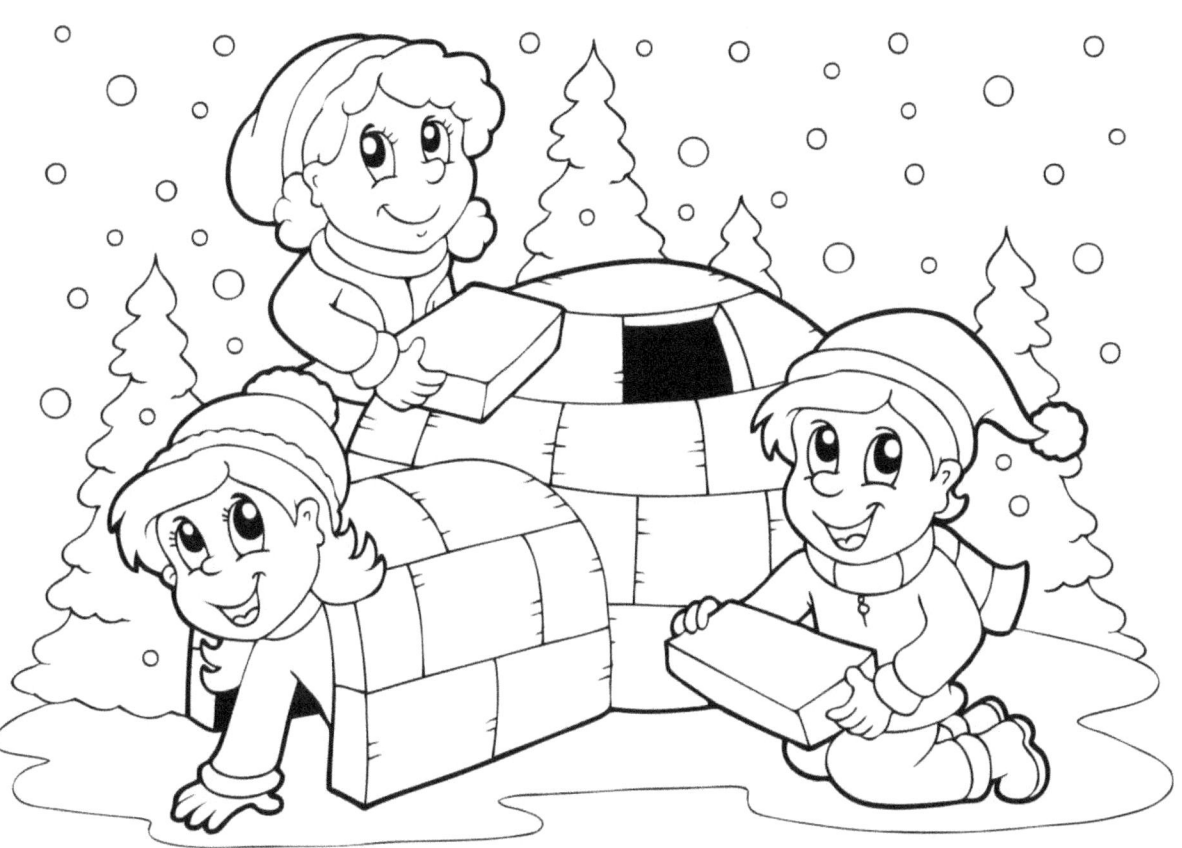

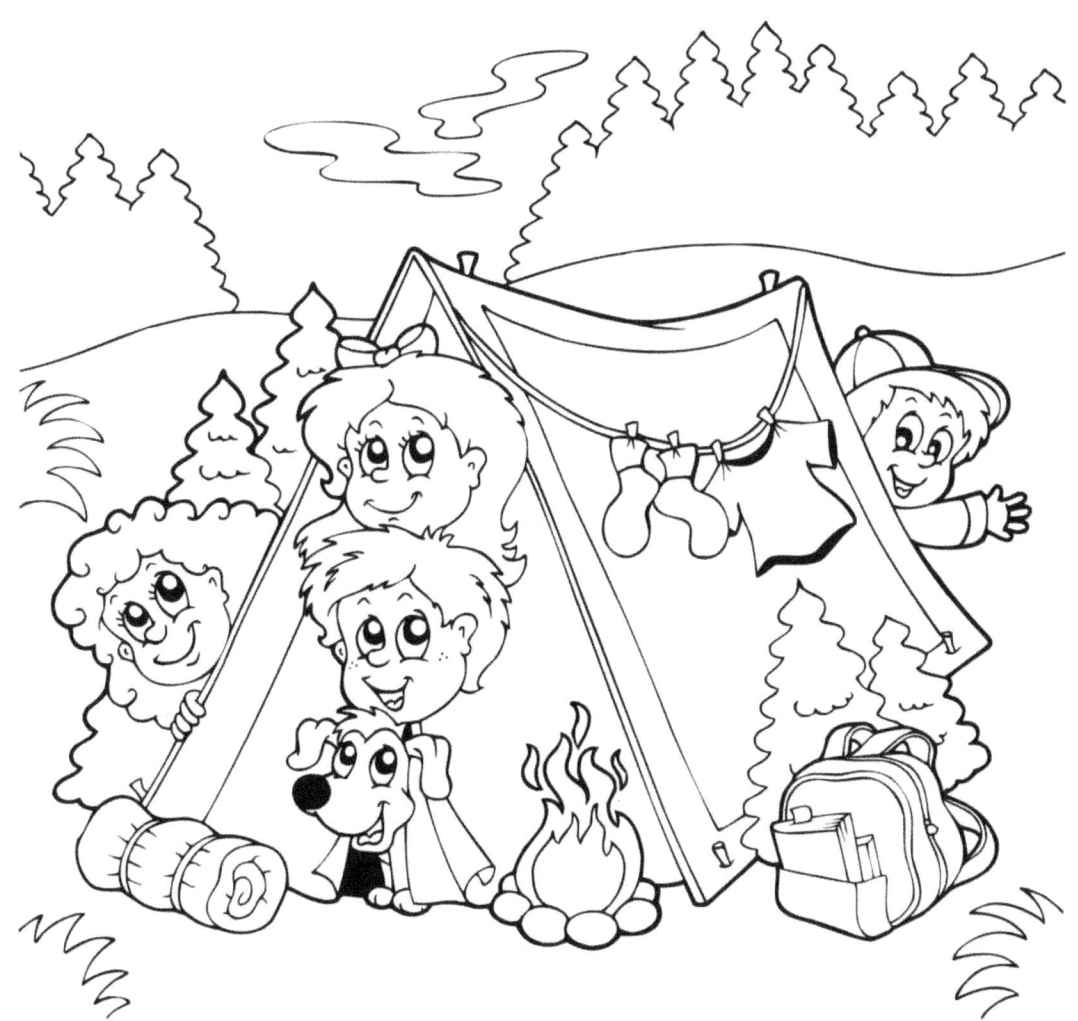

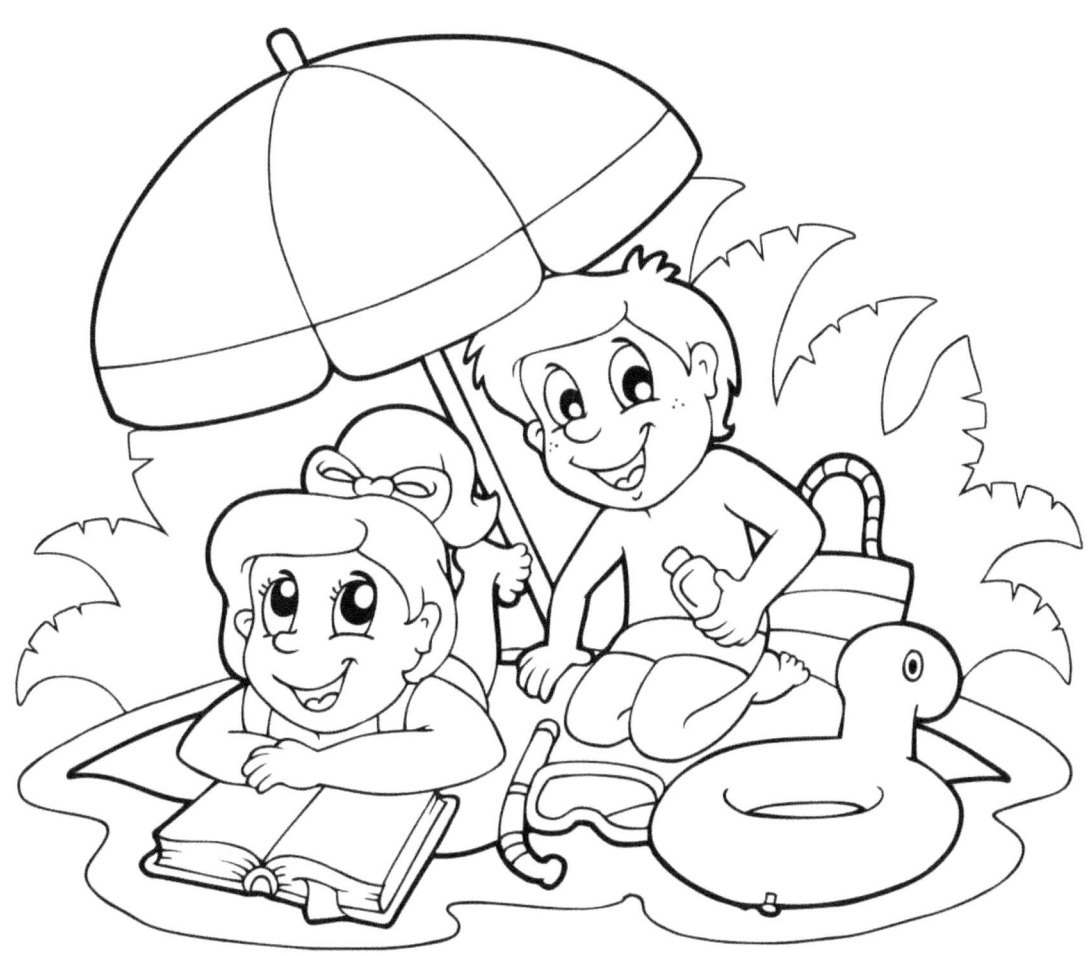

Thank you for purchase

Please share your work and see another idea
at

http://bit.ly/corruption_coloring

www.ingramcontent.com/pod-product-compliance
Lightning Source LLC
Chambersburg PA
CBHW080613190526
45169CB00007B/2993